SUPERPOWER SWITCH

Steven Butler

Pictures by
Bill Ledger

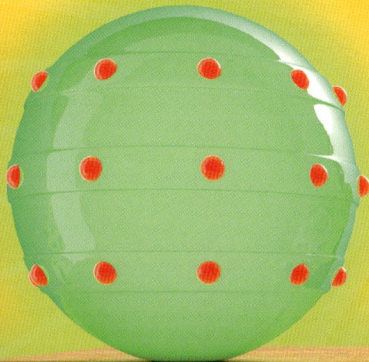

OXFORD
UNIVERSITY PRESS

Great Clarendon Street, Oxford, OX2 6DP,
United Kingdom

Oxford University Press is a department of the University of Oxford.
It furthers the University's objective of excellence in research, scholarship,
and education by publishing worldwide. Oxford is a registered trade mark of
Oxford University Press in the UK and in certain other countries

First published 2018
This edition published 2020

British Library Cataloguing in Publication Data

Data available

9780192776075

1 3 5 7 9 10 8 6 4 2

Paper used in the production of this book is a natural, recyclable product
made from wood grown in sustainable forests. The manufacturing process conforms
to the environmental regulations of the country of origin.

Printed in China

Acknowledgements
Illustrations by Bill Ledger
Activities by Karra McFarlane
Design by James W Hunter
Photo assets supplied by shutterstock.com, cgtrader.com, turbosquid.com.

CONTENTS

Helping your child to read

Before they start

- Talk about the back cover blurb. Ask your child how the friends might feel when their superpowers are swapped.
- Look at the front cover. Talk about what superpower the character on the cover might have.

During reading

- Let your child read at their own pace – don't worry if it's slow. They could read silently, or read to you out loud.
- Help them to work out words they don't know by saying each sound out loud and then blending them to say the word, e.g. *p-ow-er, power*.
- If your child still struggles with a word, just tell them the word and move on.
- Give them lots of praise for good reading!

After reading

- Look at pages 29 and 55 for some fun activities.

POWER SWAP

Steven Butler

Pictures by
Bill Ledger

In this story ...

Pip
(**BOOST**)

Pip is super strong! She can lift up really heavy weights, like boulders. She once lifted a skyscraper!

Jin
(**SWOOP**)

Evan
(**FLEX**)

Nisha
(**NIMBUS**)

Mrs Butterworth
(**COOK**)

1
PIP'S DISCOVERY

It was lunchtime at Hero Academy ...

"**Delicious!**" said Pip with a grin.
"I love power-pancakes."

"Hurry up, Pip," said Jin. "I can't wait to beat you at turbo-tennis!"

Pip smiled. She was the best in the school at turbo-tennis. "Just one more pancake," she said.

"We'll see you at the turbo-tennis court,"
Jin said. He put his dirty plate away and
went into the sunshine with Nisha and Evan.

Pip was the only one left in the dinner hall.
She gobbled down the rest of her pancake.

Pip had just finished when Mrs Butterworth
appeared.

"Would you mind helping me clear away the tables, Pip?" Mrs Butterworth asked.

Pip wanted to go and join her friends, but she knew she could use her super-strength to get the job done quickly. She smiled. "Of course I'll help, Mrs Butterworth."

"Thank you," Mrs Butterworth replied. She headed off into the kitchen.

Pip stacked four tables, one on top of the other. Then she picked the whole pile up and marched across the dinner hall. "I'll be outside having fun with the others in no time," she said to herself.

Then, quite suddenly, Pip slipped on a strawberry that had fallen off Jin's plate.

She skidded along the floor and ...
CRASH! She smashed straight through
a wall, landing in a pile of dust and
broken bricks.

Pip stood up and looked around. She
was in a room she'd never seen before.

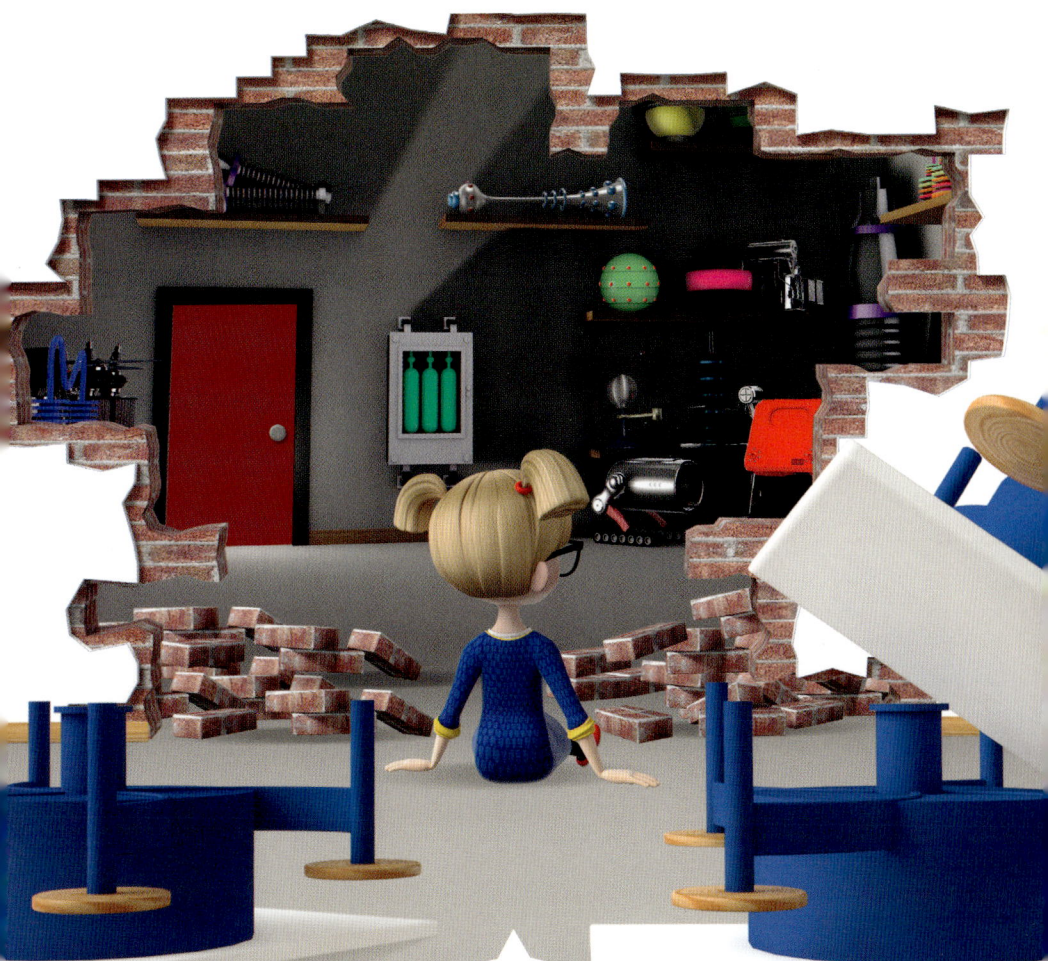

The room was filled with strange gadgets, all **BLEEPING**, **FLASHING** and TICKING.

Pip gasped when she realized where she was. It was the **Confiscated Gadgets Storeroom**. Pupils were strictly not allowed inside.

CONFISCATED GADGETS STOREROOM

The Confiscated Gadgets Storeroom is where the Head puts all the gadgets he has taken from baddies over the years.

Most dangerous gadget: the **Time Wobbler** – used by Mr Minute to time-travel.

Most mysterious gadget: **Gadget Number 261** – taken from Colonel Cortex in Egypt ten years ago. The Head is still trying to discover what it actually does.

Silliest gadget: the **Hover Umbrella** – with its spinning spokes, it can spin you around in the air until you're helpless with laughter.

2

SUPERPOWER SWAP

"I should get out of here," Pip said to herself. She turned to go, but then she spotted a green, flashing ball on one of the shelves. It was covered in little buttons and was making an odd humming sound. "Ooooooooh. I wonder what this does," she said, reaching out towards it.

As she touched it, there was a sudden **FLASH** of green light and a loud *ZING!*

Pip went flying back through the hole in the wall and landed in the middle of the dinner hall with a bump. The flashing ball fell out of her hands and rolled across the floor.

"Ugh, what happened?" Pip mumbled. Her skin tingled.

Jin ran into the dinner hall. "**AAARGH!**" he shouted. "What's going on?" Jin started to **stretch** across the room like a rubber band.

Pip rubbed her eyes. Stretching wasn't Jin's superpower!

"Something's wrong!" Evan yelled, as he flew through the air and almost crashed into Jin.

"**Evan, you can't fly!**" Pip shouted, scrambling to her feet.

"I know," Evan said, as he **WHIZZED** past.

"I've got Evan's power, and he's got mine!" said Jin, **stretching** this way and that.

Pip felt a strange CRACKLE around her hands. She looked down and saw little sparks of lightning coming out of her fingers.

"**Lightning?**" Pip said. "It's Nisha that can control weather ... not me!"

Nisha burst through the door with a look of shock on her face. The door smashed into the wall and giant cracks appeared.

"I'm super strong!" Nisha yelled. "What's going on?" She picked up a stack of chairs and gasped. "Pip, I've got your power!"

3

PIP'S LIGHTNING FINGERS

"**HELP!**" Evan shouted as he bumped his head on the ceiling.

"I can't stop **stretching!**" Jin yelled. His arm **stretched** all the way down the corridor, out of the door, and then back in through a window.

"I'll stop you!" Pip said.

Pip tried to grab Jin's arm, but a storm cloud appeared above her head and started to rain on her.

Pip gasped. "It's that gadget," she said, turning towards the glowing ball. "It must have swapped all of our powers."

Just then, a blizzard of snow shot out of her fingers.

"Make some lightning, Pip," Nisha said. "Zap the ball, quick!"

Pip watched as lots of tiny sparks raced over her hands. Having someone else's power felt so strange. What if she couldn't control it?

Pip concentrated hard and saw lightning **CRACKLING** between the tips of her fingers. "Stand back, everyone," she called.

Nisha picked up a table to use as a shield. "You can do it, Pip," she said to her friend.

Pip aimed at the glowing ball. **ZAPPPPPPP!** An ENORMOUS bolt of lightning shot from her hand and hit the gadget with a massive **BOOOOM!**

The glowing ball cracked in two and a *flash* of green light filled the dinner hall.

"*Aaargh!*" Evan tumbled to the ground.

"**Ooof!**" Jin's arms whipped back to normal.

"**Whoops!**" Nisha dropped the table she'd been holding.

4
BACK TO NORMAL

For a moment, nobody spoke. The four friends looked at each other with wide eyes.

"Did that really just happen?" Jin asked.

"I think so," Pip replied, picking up the table that Nisha had dropped. "At least I have my own power back now."

That afternoon, Pip helped Magnus fix
the hole in the wall.

Afterwards, she headed outside to meet
Jin, Nisha and Evan.

"Now can we play turbo-tennis?"
she asked.

Pip smiled as her friends ran off to the turbo-tennis courts.

"I'll let them win," she said to herself, with a grin. "Just this once!"

AFTER READING ACTIVITIES

QUICK QUIZ

See how fast you can answer these questions!
Look back at the story if you can't remember.

1) What food does Pip eat at the beginning of the story?

2) What is the name of the room that Pip smashes into?

3) Whose powers does Nisha get?

THINK ABOUT IT!

Whose powers would you most like to have? Why?

SPOT THE DIFFERENCE

Spot the four differences between the pictures of Boost.

29

OUT OF CONTROL

Steven Butler

Pictures by
Bill Ledger

In this story ...

Jin **(SWOOP)**

Jin has the power to fly. He once had a race with a jumbo jet ... and won! He can fly high enough to reach outer space!

Evan **(FLEX)**

Cam **(SWITCH)**

Nisha **(NIMBUS)**

Mr Trainer **(TEACHER)**

1
SUPER-SKILLS

"Watch me, Mr Trainer!" shouted Jin.

Jin spun into his superhero costume and became Swoop. The class were doing PE (Power Exploration), and Swoop wanted to show off his skills.

"OK, Swoop," said Mr Trainer. "Let's see what you can do!"

"Stand back, everyone," Swoop said excitedly.

Swoop shot into the sky like a rocket.

"**Wheeeeeeee!**" he shouted, as he looped around a cloud in a huge circle.

Swoop wanted to be top of the class this week. The student with the highest marks was going to receive a gold Hero Academy merit badge.

WHOOOOOSH

Swoop grinned to himself. He could already imagine the gold merit badge pinned on his uniform.

Swoop **WHIZZED** around the sports ground, and ZOOMED through the holo-hoops and under the power-poles. He landed right in front of his classmates.

"**WOW!**" Flex yelled.

"That was **terrific!**" shouted Switch.

Swoop felt like he might BURST with pride. Surely he'd win the gold merit badge?

"Well done," said Mr Trainer. "Now, who's next?"

"Me! Me! Me!" everyone shouted.

Swoop watched his friends show off their super-skills. Switch turned into a cheetah and sprinted around the school.

Then Nimbus conjured up a snow storm.

Swoop was starting to feel less and less confident that he would win the gold merit badge. His friends' super-skills were **TERRIFIC**. He had to do something more amazing if he wanted to come top of the class.

2

HIGHER AND HIGHER

Swoop marched in front of the group.

"I've got something else to show you," he said. "I'm going to fly higher than any hero has ever flown before."

Mr Trainer frowned. "Hang on, Swoop," he said. "You've had your turn."

Before Mr Trainer could stop him, Swoop was soaring into the air. He went **higher** and **higher**, until he started to feel dizzy.

Swoop took a deep breath and closed his eyes tightly. He didn't like to admit it, but he had always been a bit scared of heights.

"Just keep going," he whispered to himself. "Think of the gold merit badge."

Swoop opened one eye. Beneath him, Hero Academy was getting **smaller** and **smaller**.

"I'm sure to win now," he thought.

Swoop **rocketed** up, until Lexis City was far below.

"Just a bit further," he said to himself.

Swoop flew up through the clouds. He could feel the air around him getting icy cold.

WHOOOOOSH

He could see darkness above him, and the curve of Earth below.

Swoop gasped. He was almost in space!

Swoop tried to slow down, but he couldn't ... He was flying too **FAST!** He started to panic.

"**HELP!**" Swoop cried.

Just then, he heard a humming sound. As it got closer, he realized it was the rumble of an engine.

ZOOOOOOOOOOOOM

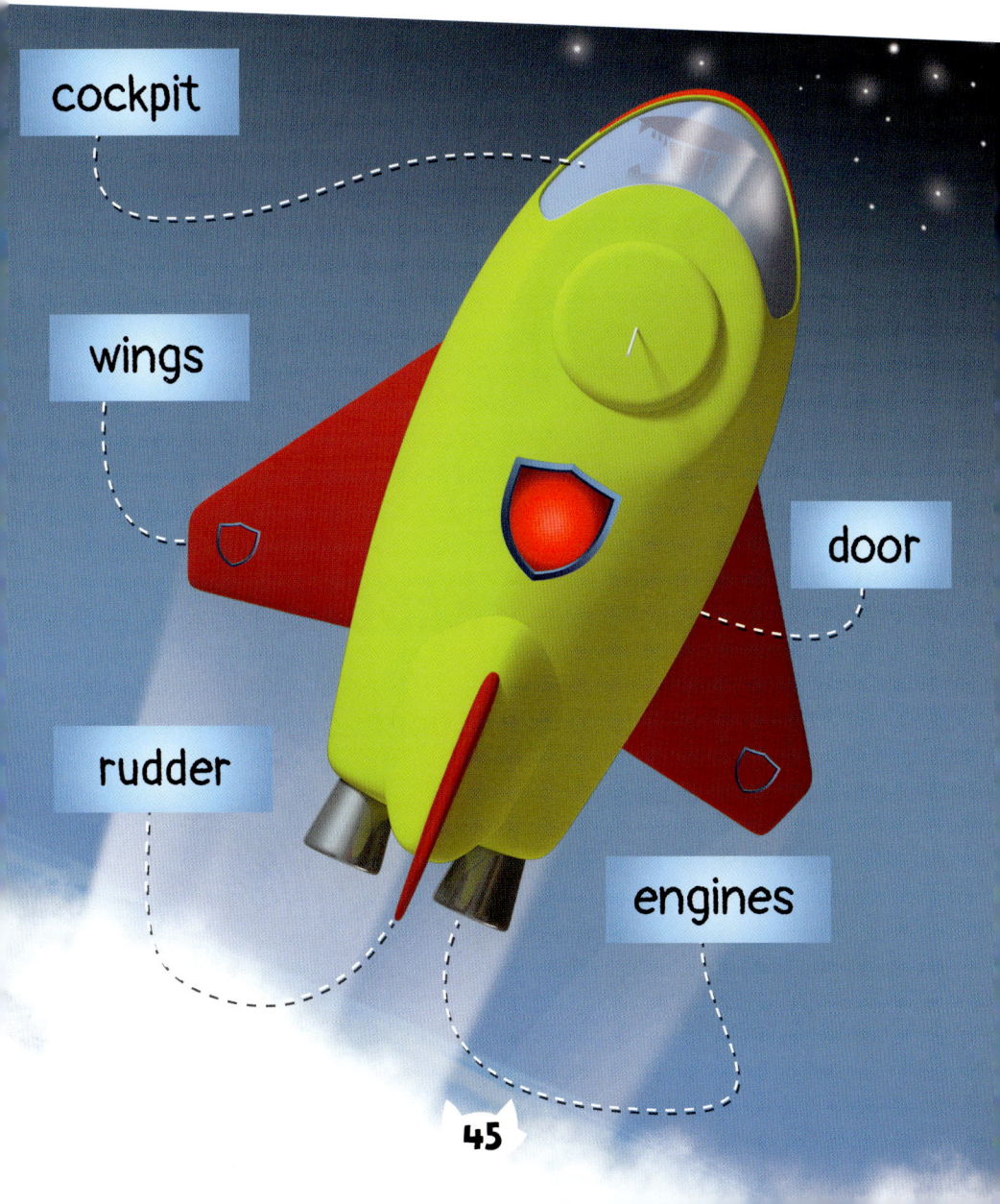

It was the Hero Academy jet!
The jet was used when the heroes
needed to go on long-distance missions.

cockpit

wings

door

rudder

engines

3

SPACE RESCUE

The hatch of the plane opened and
Mr Trainer leaned out.

"Swoop!" he shouted, over the rushing
wind. "What on earth do you think you
are doing?"

"*I can't stop!*" Swoop shouted back.

Mr Trainer slammed the hatch shut. A second later, the door opened.

"Don't panic, Swoop," a voice yelled. It was Flex. "I still haven't shown my power today."

Flex held onto the plane door with one hand and stretched out towards Swoop.

"**Please hurry!**" Swoop shouted. He was getting **further** and **further** away from the jet. In only a few more moments, he'd be lost in outer space forever.

"**Got you!**" Flex grabbed Swoop by the ankle and yanked him back towards the jet.

The two boys tumbled in through the open door and landed on the floor of the cabin.

Mr Trainer looked at Swoop crossly.

"Ummm ... sorry," Swoop said.

Mr Trainer raised one eyebrow. "Swoop," he said. "I'm glad you're safe, but what you did was **extremely** dangerous. You have a no-flying detention for a week."

"Yes, Mr Trainer," said Swoop. He looked down at his feet. They'd be staying firmly on the ground for a while.

4

THE GOLD MERIT BADGE

Swoop sat in silence for the rest of the journey back to Hero Academy. His heart was still pounding and his hands wouldn't stop shaking.

When the jet landed in the sports ground, Switch and Nimbus rushed to meet it.

"I just wanted to win the gold merit badge," Swoop said.

"Are you sure you're all right?"
Nimbus asked.

"I'm fine," mumbled Swoop. "Apart
from nearly getting lost in space!"

"Cheer up, Swoop," Flex said. "It's
not so bad."

"What do you mean?" asked Swoop.

"Mr Trainer just told me you broke the school record for the highest ever flight," Flex replied.

Swoop WHOOPED.

Flex blushed. "And I broke the school record for the highest hero rescue **EVER!**"

"Well done," Mr Trainer said, as he handed Flex the gold merit badge.

Swoop grinned at his friend. "You really deserve to win," he added.

"Maybe you'll get the badge next time," Flex replied.

"Maybe," said Swoop. "But I'll be practising my flying skills closer to the ground from now on!"

AFTER READING ACTIVITIES

QUICK QUIZ

See how fast you can answer these questions! Look back at the story if you can't remember.

1) What does the hero with the highest marks receive?
2) What does Nimbus do to show off her super-skills?
3) Who is inside the Hero Academy jet?

THINK ABOUT IT!

How does Swoop feel when Flex rescues him?

IMAGINE IT

What would you do if you had the power to fly?

Answers: 1) a gold merit badge; 2) conjures up a snow storm; 3) Mr Trainer and Flex.